Between
One Future
and the Next

Ruth Daigon

papier-
mache

Papier-Mache Press
Watsonville, CA

ISBN: 0-918949-66-1 Softcover
ISBN: 0-918949-67-X Hardcover

Cover art, "Wading Woman," © by William Chaiken
Cover design by Cynthia Heier
Photo by Tom Daigon

Grateful acknowledgment is made to the following publications which first published some of the material in this book:
Tamarack Review, Issue 64, 1974, Canada, for "Penicillin"; *Greenhouse Review*, Vol. 2, No. 1, 1979 for "A Temporary Visitor"; *Modus Operandi*, Vol. 10, No. 7, 1979 for "Family Portrait"; *Bellingham Review*, Vol. 3, No. 2, 1980 for "Not Yet Visible"; *The Poetry Review*, Vol. 1, No. 1 (Poetry Society of America, 1983) for "Point of View"; *Calliope*, Vol. 17, No. 1, 1984 for "How Old Would You Be"; *Voices* (The Poetry Society of Israel, 1986) for "Anniversary"; *Kansas Quarterly*, Vol. 19, No. 3, 1987 for "Back"; *Alaska Quarterly*, Vol. 8, Nos. 3 and 4, 1990 for "Over My Shoulder"; *The National Poetry Competition Winners* (Chester H. Jones Foundation, 1990) for "Like an Ideal Tenant"; *First Person*, Winter 1990, No. 2 for "I'd Like to Color Myself Calm"; *Snake Nation*, Issue 8, 1990 for "Sudden and Still"; *The Sow's Ear*, Fall/Winter 1990–91 for "This Town"; *Ledge*, Vol. 2, No. 3, 1991 for "Inventions"; *Pearl*, Spring/Summer 1991, No. 13, for "Eve's Legacy"; *Santa Clara Review*, Vol. 78, No. 3, 1991 for "Search"; *Free Lunch*, Winter 1992, No. 4 for "Slamming the Score Shut"; *Pearl*, Spring/Summer 1992, No. 13 for "Stung"; *Zone 3*, Vol. 6, No. 3, 1992 for "Every Herring"; *Folio*, Spring 1993 for "Intrusions"; *Green Fuse*, Spring/Summer 1993, No. 18, for "Promise"; *Green's Magazine*, Vol. XXI, No. 1, 1993, Canada for "Inventions"; *Hudson Valley Echoes*, Issue No. 28, 1993 for "Ordinary"; *If I Had My Life to Live Over I Would Pick More Daisies* (Papier-Mache Press, 1993) for "It Is Enough"; *Iowa Woman*, Spring/Summer 1993, No. 15, Vol. 13 for "Fox"; *Life on the Line* (Negative Capability, 1993) for "Outer Edge"; *Plainsongs*, Vol. 14, No. 1, 1993 for "Miracle"; *Poet & Critic*, Vol. 24, No. 3, 1993 for "Night Song"; *Visions International*, No. 42, (Black Buzzard Press, 1993) for "Priority Mail"; *Color Wheel*, No. 8, 1994 for "Fuel"; *Footworks, The Patterson Literary Review* (Passaic County Community College, 1994) for "Driftwood Days"; *Green Fuse*, No. 18, Spring/Summer 1994 for "Sunday Fishing"; *Calliope*, Vol. 17, No. 2, 1994 for "Quiet As Sand"; *Negative Capability*, 1994 for "The Moon Inside"; *Poet Lore*, Vol. 89 , No. 1, 1994 for "Running for His Life"; *Rockford Writers Guild*, Vol. 13, No. 3, 1994 for "What Happens"; *Tikkun*, Vol. 9, No. 5, 1994 for "Carpenter"; *Xavier*, Vol. 14, No. 1, 1994 for "Perspectives"; *Zone 3*, Vol. 9, No. 1, 1994 for "Basic"; *Sonoma Mandala*, Vol. 21, 1994–95 for "An Old Story"; and *Voices* (The Golden West College, 1994–95) for "A Fresh Cadence."

Library of Congress Cataloging-in-Publication Data

Daigon, Ruth.
      Between one future and the next / Ruth Daigon.
          p.   cm.
      ISBN 0-918949-66-1 (softcover : acid-free paper). — ISBN
0-918949-67-X (hardcover : acid-free paper)
      I. Title.
PS3554.A2887B47   1995
811'.54—dc20   94-38906
                                                                     CIP

To all the people who inhabit this book
especially Artie, Tom, and Glenn

Contents

One eye sees, the other feels
—Paul Klee

What More

In a pause between
one future and the next
we enter stepping lightly

and move through air
like a weather vane
turning on its swivel.

Like a bird in sudden lifts
we explore a steady
stream of horizons

a day of passing sky
consenting light   a sound
with silence of its own.

And if the wind is right
we lift our arms

and fly.

Snow

We sleep beside the body of morning
until sunlight unveils a white world.

Like geometric moments in flight
flake by flake by flake drifts
down in furred silence.

Snow settles on our shoulders.
Crystal cobwebs hang from trees.
A wordless white lies underfoot.

We walk through unexplored woods,
join fresh tracks of animals,
make compacts with the climate

as though this northern reach—
snow streaked, wind worn—
were all that's left of the earth.

Wrapped in a dream of snow,
we never want to leave
this Siberia of the mind.
The weather's calm beyond forecast,

air carefully constructed.
We can hear the earth turning,
certain we're the only ones.
In frost-thinned moonlight

old sounds vibrate
like tuning forks.
A twilight of voices hums
inside us like a second heart

and the dead musicians
breathe in our ears
love songs, birth songs,
death songs.

All the melodies
we left behind
return and take us
back in their arms.

Moment

In the mind of winter
it's been cold a long time
and the north wind blows
in the same bare place.

The sun skids on frozen
surfaces, and fog
chokes off all sound.

The eye blots out
images of seedlings, finds
peace in brittle landscapes
and comfort in bare limbs.

A snowflake resting
in a child's palm
makes her life
a simple moment.

This moment,
emptied of all memories
but one.

Snapshots

The camera stores the hours when
everything returns to the right hand,
viewfinder matching patterns
of parents and children, shutter
measuring different speeds of dying,

flash fixing days when the living
came together with remembered
sounds of hammers pounding
nails, hands slapping dough,
sticks rattling fences.

Everything stored in an eye flash.
All the parts reconciled
in a landscape with grass
a shade that never was.
Nothing realized, but certain
and just about to happen.

Back where absence begins, we're
searching for a sunset shot,
inventing endings that come out
right, waiting for negatives
yet to be developed.

Family Portrait

One face anchored in its smile,
the other curtained in itself,
my picture parents, I can
barely see you now as you
bleach into this document.

You were the first to understand distance,
leaving a pause between two sighs,
a slight murmur in the blood.
This photograph of you is like
a clock bending time—

an instant transformed into crystal
between my chalk-ridden fingers—
and whatever whitened inside you
like a bone or a guardian angel
is etched in the palm of my hand.

Carpenter

Before the dream evaporates,
the paint flakes or fades,
my father sheathed in calluses
hefts the hammer and
pounds each nail into
its proper place, making
sound music from sound noise.

His days hinge together.
Mornings he wakes early,
shakes the furnace down, and
opens dampers so the fire
blazes as she squeezes juice,
cooks porridge, and listens
to those noisy seven overhead.

A building permit's his safe-
conduct to the future
where he's a weekend
revolutionary—reads *The Daily
Worker* and saws and hammers outside
in the winter with his union card
warming his vest pocket.

When his sander strips time
down to its clean edge, he
leaves the city weekends
to soak in the lake or
sit in the sun building sand
castles with his children.

He looks for structural fatigue
in his marriage. With her
it's always twenty below.
The weather has its reasons
and so does she (always busy),
sweeping her days free of his sawdust,
her nights of his fingerprints.

His drill digs deep
exposing the bitter past:
mother dead and he apprenticed
to a carpenter at nine,
the ocean crossing and the stench
of steerage when he was seventeen,
laying railroad tracks
and sleeping in unheated boxcars
until a worker froze.

His miter box builds secrecy
of corners. There, he hides
his mandolin, strums it
with his amputated finger
or switches off the buzz saw
to hear silence grow.

His wedge separates the hours, pries
a little extra time into his life—
a chance to listen to Caruso
after supper, play a game of
checkers, or hum light opera gems.

His ruler measures out our
jump-rope days until each
hour expands. His sharp eye
and a T square keep us level.
And when he stops his work
to wave, we all wave back.

His saw crosscuts the years.
He hears his children
singing, smells the scent
of wood shavings and glue,
wakes each morning
and feels his pulse beat fast.

His screwdriver tightens
tendons, ligaments, and bones
that give him strength
to build our house from memory,
and deep in the house's heart
he makes a room for each of us
with a window's width of light.

Now, we're safe inside our simple
rooms in our simple house
with his sandpapered arms
wrapped tight around us
as if time were nothing at all.

Poppy Seed Cookies

you come in from the cold
warm your hands   the air
glows golden with the smell
of her sweet dough browning

a glass of cool milk
on the clean table
her cookies fresh from the pan
poppy seeds spattering
each perfect circle

you take one in each hand
crunch them slowly
wet your fingers
mopping up crumbs

once her words tasted
bitter as yeast
on the tongue
now the distance
between you is gone

she's close by baking cookies
the sun in her apron pocket
you are partners again
like a batch of dough
and the rolling pin

this is the dream you have been
dreaming all your life

The Moon Inside

1

Women know how to wait.
They smell the dust,
listen to light bulbs dim,
and guard the children
pale with dreaming.

They hear danger
tapping along walls,
sidewalks sinking,
and edges of the city

bruising the landscape.
Down long corridors
they whisper to each other
of alarm bells

and balanced crosses,
of shrouded eyes and empty stars
while the moon inside them
takes a slow, silver breath.

2

She keeps pulling him up
from the bottom of the Red River
in stop action or slow motion
and replays the splash
blooming around his hips.

She corrects his dive,
restores the promise
of his form, each movement
clear in the instant of falling.

The moment reversed,
she reels him up
to where he's still
sitting on the bank.

Now, she covers her scalp
with hair torn by its roots.
Screams sucked back into her mouth
become soft syllables again.

Her shredded clothes are rewoven,
the table set for his return.

3

As the body's laid out,
she stands at attention
waiting for the clearest light
and then sharpens her instruments.

First, the eyes removed
to see what was seen,
ears probed to hear what was heard,
then the heart dissected
to find what was missing.

It takes time to cut tenderly
into the bone and sinew
of the past,
each knife stroke
a loving incision.

There is no entrance,
only entering.
When the body's
exposed,
she climbs inside,
pulls closed the flaps of skin,
and slowly heals herself.

4

In her kitchen, she knows
each blunted blade,
worn handle, broken tip—
the past compressed in steel.

Along with sacramental noise of
cups knocking, lips smacking,
she hears carving knives and cleavers
splitting days into edible proportions.

Skillful at the cutting board,
she pays her vegetable tithes
to the crock pot, the salad,
the wok, slices and slices
into the heart of things.

Familiar knives carve her into
chunks served up for family supper.
From the scraps and bones
she makes a broth and feeds herself.

5

She lay sprawled on the table
between a pitcher of milk
and a stained napkin. A giant
sponge swept her crumbling parts
over the edge. Before dis-
appearing into the dustpan,
she remembered how simple
life had been between the curved
fork and serrated knife.

6

Nineteen thirty was a long,
cold childhood wedged into a scar
and food that filled half
the cupboard. She licked
the pencil stump and
made her lists. Each
item considered, written,
erased, rewritten
according to what jingled
in the broken teapot.

At six o'clock, she always
listened to the news and groaned,
her body a vast burial ground for
victims of plagues, revolutions,
wars, each groan another corpse.
She stood ironing, every stroke
a preparation for the burial,
a straightening of limbs,
a smoothing of features,
a final act of love.

7

A convention of women facing out
into the lens,
picnics
birthdays,
all swimming to the surface
of the acid bath—
a procession of cardboard moments
poorly focused
with here and there
an empty space
like a prediction.

Winter Wash

she wakes and touches
hard bones of sleep
her heart thuds permanent
and fast between the sheets

she draws the blinds
and lets light come in
a frozen slice of morning

hands gnawed by frost
she hangs out sheets
wind lays cold transparent
palms against her cheeks

she washes dishes   replaces bulbs
finds keys   and waits in quiet rooms
for days to settle and wash to dry

she sits and sifts through hours
fearful she might go blind or
lose herself beyond repair

watching sun-bleached linen
sailing into a sea-blue sky
and in her wild imaginings
beyond this cage of time

there is her horizon of clean sheets
there the air between them
there her thoughts blow free

Names

Sunday nights at seven he
sits at the kitchen table,
picks the largest apple in the bowl,
and with something older than patience,
he begins the silent, ritual peeling.

His knife makes a quick incision
back into the past. We sit as
they sat long ago, waiting for
apples to be stripped, cored,
sprinkled with cinnamon.

He scrapes away the soft spots
making the fruit perfect while
we wind each spiral through
our fingers and inhale the fragrance
of familiar names.

Noah, words shooting from
the sharp edge of his tongue.
David, swimming deep enough to drown.
Riva, smiles crackling like old parchment.
Sonya, Sam, Reuven, Gitl.

Names heavy with old weather.
Names calling like train whistles in the dark.
Names smelling of strange earth
where they have been and gone from
and which we will never
know as we watch our uncle
peeling back the layers of our lives.

Missing

We're still waiting,
less radiant, less sure.
It grows dark.
We light candles.

Cousins,
strange in serious suits,
fold their hands and sing
old, familiar songs.

Sleep.
Sleep.
The grass is growing
and a single bird tests the air
reminding us today is all there is.

Sleep.
Sleep.
The grass is growing
and the well's not deep enough
to drown the moon.

Light condenses.
Doors swing open
but the guest is
not yet visible.

The dream still in our mouths,
we drift to a room
where the thin gruel of
early morning light

falls on a scarred table-
top and a white plate
with its burden
of black bread.

Now we keep very still
and wait for the missing one
to come again and share
this heavy loaf of silence.

Anniversary

When our family sat down to measure time,
space opened wide. Unhinged doors, uprooted
furniture was propped against the walls
like fat observers making room for naked
planks that served as tables for tonight
and building frames tomorrow. We needed
large accommodations when our family
sat down to measure time. We tallied it
by heartbeats and periods of hunger.
The handmade cloth transposed wooden planks.
Platters overflowed on gold embroidered threads.
Words streamed through wax and burning sand
past bells and moving pointers tooth by
tooth at intervals in memory of the dead
when our family sat down to measure time.

A Typical Manitoba
Railroad Station

I can still feel the slivers
as I slid on the platform, restless,
waiting for those weekend
guests. We hiked the mile back

from the depot, took the shortcut
across Thorkelson's field or the long
way round over hedge, ditch, road
raw with skid marks and sunlight.

The sun was a piece of bait to get us
up in the morning. Nothing stirred
except a grasshopper clinging to a
blade weighing it toward its roots.

Too cold for swimming, we marched
along railroad ties, careful
not to miss a single one or
we had to pay a forfeit.

Lonesome for the whistle,
we waited for a train
and when none appeared,
we watched the tracks.

Stuck in our skins, we
sat on the ties studying the dirt
under our nails with our life-
lines buried in our fists.

Quick As Overnight

We'd crowd around the fireplace
listening for spring
and no green was as green
as the color of last year.

Then, quick as overnight it was spring
and underneath
a silence of rocks melting
in the Red and the Assiniboine.

When the sun inched up
we ran down dirt roads
or lay in the shade watching
forests shoot between our fingers.

At night we listened to sounds
prowling through the dark.
Eyes shut, hands folded
we practiced dying until
light prodded us awake.

Now, tones thin as reeds
stroke our ears,
echoes of windows nailed shut
waves of parents washing away
names refusing to let go.

We sort them, separate them
store them in earth
shards for diggers yet to come.

Not Me

This is not the way I really am.
I'm thinner, younger.
But yesterday I cut my hair
and now my early loves dissolve
behind my eyes
leaving a few wrinkles.

If you follow the dotted lines
they will lead you to me.
I am the shyness of my mother
preparing her first child,
the boldness of my father
leaving Europe behind.

I've inherited their tools:
his stubborn hammer,
her patient needle
lie ready to my hand.

I am not of my clothes
nor the sound of my voice.
It's been cracked by family quarrels
long before I was born.
Even my eyes still reflect
my grandmother in prayer.

When you look for me
I'll be the one
waving the banner,
Not Guilty.

Slamming the Score Shut

I'm slamming the score shut,
tired of all the arias
they've given me. Everything's
marked *loud   soft*
sung with feeling or restraint.

I would like to sing with
meaning, spit consonants like
Mr. Saidman spit pumpkin seeds
right between his upper
and his lower plate,
a real professional.

Let's buy another bag of seeds
Mr. Saidman. You can sing them
in your bass, I in my soprano.
We'll cover all the streetcar
tracks on Selkirk Avenue
until it looks like snow.

You and I, Mr. Saidman,
make a music held together
by the husks and seeds
of immigrants that never
learned to read a score.

Friday

Friday happens all at
once. It wakes with soft
stirrings and floats toward
the husk of day.

Friday tastes of apples
and slivered almonds crunched
slowly, the snick of seeds
against tongues as juice
trickles down.

Friday serenades with
violins and fresh counterpoints
of sound, a day of cool
amazement, deep breathing,
and litanies of light.

On Friday, children
leave school early, mothers
wax floors and bake
poppy seed cookies.

Friday is a river of
small shapes, snowmelt, sun-
streaks, and palm-smooth winds.

After climbing Friday's
tree, you can perch on
the highest branch and
all the astonishments will
wrap around you.

Intrusions

The birds are at it again.
Someone's wound them up
and their calls spiral around us.
Light swings open its door
and the wind says nothing new.

The morning moon's still hanging
in the saffron sky and
as the newest season melts,
leaves release the light
they stored all winter.

Spears of grass make
delicate intrusions, and water
sucks at its own edge. Since
we're the first to wake
it all belongs to us.

In rooms filling with daylight it's
best to keep still, lie close
to the quick, and wait for spring
slipping in surefooted just before dawn
with fur and feathers in its mouth.

Flight

wings
more silent than breath
trees
riddled with stunned beginnings
a beak
tapping through a shell
a wafer of sound
and a cluster of puff and feathers

birds hanging on drafts
embroider the air
with sequins of sound

hours thick with sun and seeds
a sky
all swoop and soar
as parents
in shapes of tenderness
wheel back to the nest

that's how it is with them

feeding the young
teaching them to fly

the horizon flushed with flight
a few small bodies on the ground
and the day heavy with old business

wrentit
red-whiskered bulbul
melodious grassquit
or stub-winged sparrow

all content to find the crumb
the bug
not size but surge
makes them fly
quick wings
swimming through rivers of sky

and never short of wonder

The Planting

When sun slashes open morning,
she walks out barefoot,
and if her feet were not half
buried in garden soil,
she might be floating as
easily as falling in a dream.

Like the oldest gardener
digging the oldest garden,
she plants last year's tubers
six inches deep, one foot
apart, fertility the width
of her dirt-stained thumb.

Sun rests on her shoulder
warm as her father's hand.
She remembers light slicing
through the kitchen where
the rubber plant stood—

Mother scrubbing its leaves;
Brother, his hair bladed like
new grass, pushing the plant
from one sun strip to another;
the whole family wrapped in a
gauze of sleep.

Cool spaces gather under
the table. Sudden lilacs fall
loosely into summer where
pages of the past stack up
like old seed catalogues.
A spasm of light returns her

to the warm-skinned sky, air
thick and sweet as maple sap.
After tamping down earth, she
shakes dirt from her hands,
straightens her back, straddles
the furrow, and opens her palms
to the sun's hot kiss.

Parlez-Moi D'Amour

Although your accent's
strange to my ears, we
share a common language.
I've absorbed your idiom,
become fluent in your tongue
and familiar with your grammar.
Even when your rhythm runs
counterpoint to mine, we
move in concert as quick as
juice in power lines,
insertions in each other's
speech—mine the story,
yours the ending, mine
the joke, yours the punch
line. Words breed
and multiply between
your tongue and mine,
all our tender transactions
as effortless as love.

Dance

The breath comes easy
and the steps are long.
Streamlined by rhythm,
fed by energy of hips and hair
we swing across the floor.

Once, I chalked soliloquies
on sidewalks, danced
without a partner.
Now, I know your rhythms
even in your sleep, the way
you punch your pillow,
find a cooler space,
shift from side to side.

We move in hesitations
the way desire works
on the heart. You hold me
like a bar chord to the melody
of muscle, timpani of bone.

I, my mother's daughter,
you, your father's son,
move to early music,
crazy with life
as we dance along
the slipstream of the past.

When Light Was Soft
and Everywhere

we made a party
for everyone we knew
and those we never knew

drank wine
ate fruit
out of season

sat on the ground
the smell of damp
rising rich between our knees

remembered
everything we'd done
or imagined

told stories about a woman
who wore her flesh
like armor

a child who
swallowed its reflection
in the mirror

a man
whose clothes
smelled of travel

we talked
to the sound
of baroque violins

walked into rooms
our heads
sprouting ornaments

and later
went back to doing
what we always do

Swimming

The pond's a fresher blue.
Frogs leap along the edge
with a hundred night songs.

The water's tempting with its
shine, its pulse, its flow,
its promise of abandon.

She strips and enters, swimming
steadily away from herself,
one stroke at a time

and longs for things that do not
surface. Mossy sounds slip
arms around brown shoulders.

The quiet breathes in and out
of focus as she floats emerald green
on sea green under a grass green sky.

Sun fixes her with light, warms
her back and widespread legs
until she lifts her head and shouts.

Echoes skim along the water
like flat stones in wider and
wider circles. She surrenders

to the sun, the air, the current
knowing water just like love
can take her anywhere she
hasn't been before.

Sunday Fishing:
The Blues Are Running

After the boat returns,
we watch men hosing decks
slippery with scales
and eyes and blood.

The crew shows us
how to hook bait,
how to cast, how to play
the line until the catch.

It's a delicate business
knowing tug from tangle
and reeling in the fish,
a different kind of mathematics.

The sun's a shawl of burning.
Stunned by heat,
we tip bottles back
and iced beer drives
a spike through our heads.

Suddenly the pole's alive
and a sweet energy flows
up from the ocean floor.

Arching in parabolic curves,
a shape flares out of the water.
With the strength of blind love
we grip the rod and hold on.

The fish flails, teaching us
distance and direction
and the line's a tether
neither will let go.

Netted, dumped in sacks,
the dead lie intimate as lovers.
White underbellies flash
in the light, smoky bodies
darken, jagged teeth
close neatly together.

A stiffening of weather
sends us back, and everything
promised has been delivered.

Wet World

I strip and give myself
to the current in a secret
baptism. Then, swimming along
a beam of light, the sun
under my elbow, I feel

the muscle inside the water,
the surface skin. Through layers
of drowned time, my body moves
like a sleek fish so quick,
no bait can tempt me.

In this wet world, I swim
back and forth, back and forth,
now into the willow's shadow,
now into the light,
exchanging shade for shade.

Between me and the shore,
whispers skim along the water—
creak of tree, scrub of brush.
Summer lasts forever.

I think of air and float,
think of earth and still
float, the skin-warm
liquid washing me

then I move by touch alone,
feel the water pour its meaning
through my hands, and know
exactly who I am.

Swimming in Air

Every herring hangs by its own head
        —Thomas Carlyle

After they string you up,
you open your gills
like a blessing,
a gasp of unity
with all the others
trapped in the same net.

Wrapped in your sheen
with your fish mouth
and unshuttered eye,
you splash in waves of wind
to the rhythm of remembered water.

Parsing darkness with your finny smell,
you learn the shape of dry space
as the liquid life
shimmers down below.

But everything that cannot swim
begins to drown in sunlight.
Your journey shrinks
as you shrivel.

When evening nails down the day,
you hang cluttering the cool night,
splintering darkness, and leaping
at the moon's white thumbnail.

Again

I sleep with one eye open
and I have everywhere
to lay my head.

Time has its own country
where I take long walks
and tie my laces tight.

Plump with the unknown
and ripe with secrets,
I love what's easy.

Shadows link and lie down
one by one, and stars obey
night's small rehearsal.
When birds screech the dawn

I awaken to moist morning,
the patience of my tree,
the curiosity behind my fence.

A bulrush leads me to a lost lagoon.
A feather floats me to the edge of flight.
A weed points me to my roots.

Then I shout up to the sun,
old fireball, old father,
It's you again.

Harvest

We harvest a crop of babies
whose thighs and bellies
fill the cribs of our house.

We hold their small wonder,
their child smell,
kiss their eyes,
praise their noise,
and shield them from the dark.

When we take them by the hand
our fingers fuse
to make piecings
in a miracle of edges.

They begin their play
and disappear into
tall grass tinged
with the color of gone-by.

All things warm and
breathing remind us
of the time their sweet
breath joined with ours

and of those moments
when we knew exactly
how perfect we were.

Sudden and Still

for Betsy

Here to my hiding place bring me
succulents, honey bees, clover
to fill that vacant space,
lizards, wildflowers, shallots
to soften this brittle shell,
wine, fire opal, ripening grain
to make me fertile again.

She slept so light
hardly an imprint on the sheet
and then she rose and slipped
away disturbing no one.
Now, like an eyelash caught
in a tear duct, I keep
blinking her back.

Again it's 4 A.M.
last night's wine stain
still on the tablecloth,
moonlight coloring in
the shades of sleep.
Again the doorbell rings.
I filter the air before swallowing.

Which child is it?

But I know before knowing
and catch my breath

until the house is still
and I as motionless as she.

*How long will my hand
cool in yours?*

I keep ungluing memories
like snapshots, three-by-five moments,
carry her cubed in my palm,
turn my wrist to see
the infant, child, woman
and reach through her to lose myself.

Asleep, her father hunts for
skid marks and survivors.

I drape my life around me
like an old coat,
trace my patterns
through the house,
and climb the stairs
until I reach the hovering place
where I can say

my eyes were steady enough,
my body shelter enough,
my right arm love enough.

Time Watch

An old hunting lodge,
fifty acres, and a pond
hug nearby woods.

A mile down the road
a herd of cows is grazing
long before our time
and long after.

For the farmer it's
always 5 A.M., and he is
always milking;
his wife in the kitchen
says nothing.

A swath of blue sky
stretches over birds
hanging hard on air.
Land spreads wide and
sound runs off into silence.

I'm home alone with mirrors
on a morning like any other
morning: warm half-light,
sky gathering in windows,
sacks full of shadows in corners.

It's a short mile
down to the post office
where I send invitations
to friends in other states
we've hot water, cool nights,
warm beds, and love . . .

Back home
the rooms swept free of sleep,
I move from door to door
and know exactly
what this house can give
what it can take.

I cook the food,
feed the children
from my fingertips,
and sit at the table
watching time drip like
coffee in the percolator,
letting it cool before
raising it to my lips.

The Needle Trade

The tailor—
hunched over cutting tables—
sketched designs,
chalked fabrics

and the finisher—
her needle tracing the Polish alphabet—
basted, hemmed the fine linen,
and sewed you together.

Then, in our days of loose threads,
just as your father sewed
buttons on suits to tighten
those hanging loose,

just as your mother patched
worn fabric and mended ripped
seams where thread frayed
or came undone, you

chose the proper needle,
the strength of thread
and with such skill
stitched the two of us
together.

And we, in turn, shape
patterns of our sons until
they grasp the chalk
to craft their own designs.

Not Yet Visible

My father balances on scaffolding
high above our games.
Each time he spits a nail
and drives it in,
a wall goes up.
Room dividers rise
from hopscotch squares,
the whole house framed on stilts.

He climbs the ladder,
waves from every window
until I catch his signal,
return it, and find myself
waving from our top floor
at his bent frame growing smaller
as he moves along receding avenues.

I look out
signaling my sons
who for a moment
recognize me, signal back,
then shift into a new position
straining to see something
not yet visible.

Running for His Life

for Glenn

He wakes out of bleached sleep
and begins to run, his head
full of lights and bells.

Fog burns slowly into morning
as he sprints past a rush of flowers,
a wall's long skeleton,
trees awash with wind,
fields tangled and wild.

Warm in the cloud of his breath,
he races past the open eye
of the pond where secret mouths
are feeding. Air threads
through his lungs as he calls
the names of his uncles
out of their secret cells.

They appear and run beside him
back to where it was,
back into the spring thaw
through the hot summer
past the dried leaves of fall
into the hardpan of winter.

And in the wilderness of evening,
birds hang motionless
under a star-soaked sky
and a warm wind calls them

back to a life
several futures wide
full of children's kindergarten smiles,
parents rocking on the porch,
and someone always coming home
to all those vanished Fridays.

An Old Story

You lay smooth and oval
cushioned in dreams. We
slept with all the lights
waiting for years
to tear us loose.

We rocked you in the rain's arms
in the waves' small flow
skimmed stones along water
and listened for echoes
you would hear
twenty years from now.

You kicked the earth
where love and gravity
held everything in place.
We're learning to count
backward until nothing
has numbers anymore.

We loved you
so near the bone
it fit like a muscle,
walked with you
in small steps until you

crossed the border
with nothing to declare.
Your life was in your pocket
you could spend it anywhere.

Now we shake hands
across the kitchen table,
send you off with a smile,
a postcard and a coin,

and when you call
you talk to us
in words as natural
and deadly as love.

Priority Mail for My Sons

for Tom and Glenn

I mailed you an extra year
from another country
where wooden sidewalks
end in cinder paths

where privies lean
a little more each year
and morning light falls
weightless on rain barrels.

Enclosed you'll find a Chevy
with running boards and
a Burma-Shave sign
that points the way you'll

travel years from now.
I've wrapped with care
the smell of citronella
camphor and cod liver oil

the gramophone scratching out
hi-di-hi's and bye-bye-blues,
a blade of grass to whistle through,
a fortress at the beach

a woolen bathing suit that
shrinks an inch each season.
It's just arrived and waiting
at the back door of your life.

And It Continues

We lie together in late afternoon
while they call our names,
blow whistles, ring bells.
And the rain continues
all the way to Jerusalem.
Outside our window,
grass blades stand at attention.

Here, there is order,
a calm of pillows,
smooth sheets. We
dip into each other
to taste the ripe,
fermented juice and
channel into every curve.

I trace the pathway
of your spine,
the firm geography
of back and legs,
your choir of flesh as we
explore a world of drowning,
a silence of deep water.

We swim together in the tropics
past sunken forests and
hidden treasure
shining up from below.

Stung

On a slow moving August day,
I'm cradled in the grass,
staring at the sun's slow swing,
watching ants march single
file up a fence post.

The world walks off into space
and I'm a tourist visiting
my own life sending postcards
where everything looks lovely.

Reaching for a flower, I'm stung
and know death follows. The body
held in the palm of my hand,
wingspread fine as rice paper,
surface veined and lightly varnished,

it's hard to believe
anything so perfect
would kill itself over me.

Berry Picking in Manitoba

Raspberry time's in August
when the difference between
sun and shade grows more urgent.

We plant pails in moist earth,
reach for loaded branches, and part
them like tangled skeins of hair.

Leaving unripe berries
to drop and rot, we pluck
those rich to bursting

still warm from the sun,
rub them across our lips
to smudge in color, slip

them in our mouths,
fruit and teeth and tongue
in juicy unity.

As we strip branches,
nothing's in sight
but leaves and sky.

Brambles crosshatch arms
and the world contracts
to the bottom of a bucket.

Going home, we stop and look
back at August picked clean.

Strawberry Preserves

In the dim noon of the cellar
I locate the cupboard
where preserves are stored,
carry her last jar
up into sunlight,
brush away dust,
pry open the lid, and
breath the succulent air,
then thrust my tongue
through the jar's mouth and
taste the sweetness glazed
with August she preserved
all those wintry years.

Settlement

Yesterday I buried my hand
under leaves and compost
just where the earth turns moist.
It sank past roots
and rested among rocks,
free of air and light and me.

And that became a bedtime story
for the children,
a legend lying dormant
for a quick age or so.

Some day,
on the earliest of mornings,
the sun will sink shafts
to my long-buried hand
and draw it to the surface again.

Suddenly

Sleep strips you down
and all the little deaths
flow between us. I
lift your sleeping hand,
feel its weight rise
up into my arm, and run
my fingers down your palm,
tracing myself back into your future.

Long strands of hours
lie stitched in silence.
I'm awake with the dead
moon for company, night
clean as driftwood,
cold as stone. I fall
to the furthest tip of sleep

and wake to a morning
bright with bird feathers,
sun slanting over houses
where thin light takes hold.

In a wide and quiet emptiness,
the horizon's so far, it disappears,
the air ripe with small winds,
star jasmine gone wild,
and the marvelous machinery of dawn.

Let Me Assure You

Since I'm your everyday love,
let me assure you,
you've broken nothing that's
not been smashed before
and healed easily.

We never had a choice.
Sometimes your subtle knife
caused a few shudders
but by now, digging deeper,
it hardly hurts at all.
I also have my small resurrections

and when it's my turn
to trace your networks
until I find weak spots
and blood spatters both of us,
we are not surprised.

In the morning,
we drink our coffee and
watch the same bird
attacking its reflection
in our window
over and over.

Point of View

Love does not consist of gazing
at each other but in looking
outward in the same direction,
said Antoine de Saint Exupéry.
If that's true, then we're sunk.

Sometimes I catch sight of something
your far eye discovered long ago,
but seldom.
For me, the air burns on the horizon.
For you, it's hot.
I see tender feedings.
You see signs of spring.
I talk about the moment gone to seed.
You talk about time wasted.
I inhabit the weather.
You wear a raincoat.

But after the body's long pull
through the night
(which you call sleep),
we wake to bright buds of sound
and we're both struck dumb.

On My Side of the Bed

On my side of the bed,
the air is still and secret.
The climate nourishes
a bed of seedlings rooted in April,
a wealth of bulbs and tubers,
a garden of plump growing things,
tomatoes fleshing out on the vine,
lettuce ripening unseen,
each layer crisp and sweet
folding in freshness
of the one below.
If you tear off a leaf,
hold it firm between your lips,
you'll taste all our summers buried there.

A Fresh Cadence

awake I run my hands
along the flesh I know
better than my own
your body turns toward me
curves against my back
matching perfectly
our mouths shape words
into a new language
stored in linen
for the slow years ahead

shadows stitch the night
we are in a different country
I let my fingernails grow
paint my eyelids blue and invent
hot nights in our fifth floor
Village walk-up above Italian
shouts and smells where a thin
thread of sun hovers in a life
of fresh mornings
steamy afternoons and naked
nights dreaming of feathers

when our familiar bodies drift
toward each other we are back
in our private room with windows
where silence gathers
in a grain of sound
a fresh cadence
the open reed of the heart

Oranges

After the long hard footfirst,
come downstairs and share
an orange with me.

Leaning against the sink,
separating my half, I study
the lone plant on the sill
feel every spine of that cactus

and all my hauntings
disappear when you sit
opposite me and reach
for your half of the fruit.

Let's run our tongues
across the surface,
separate each section
without puncturing the sac.

Sucking on our halves
of an orange world,
the juice runs down
as it ran long ago,
ripe and fresh and sweet.

Everywhere Like Grass

In the other, the sunken life,
in the world of tangled roots,
it is cool and quiet, and
in beds of seedlings,
in meadows of curved stems,
our wild increase sprouting again.

The dark nourishes new growth
reaching out toward horizons
where hills are still transparent
and the ground is white with
drippings from the moon.

Waking from soft-skinned dreams,
we'll face the skirmish of each day
with hostages retrieved from the night;
this time will be different—
new patterns for the feet,
wings for the eyes,

and our names everywhere like grass.

Miracle

I wheel up and down the aisles
knowing just where to reach.
Attracted by the bland companionship
of mushrooms, fragrant freshness
of lettuce, fleshy opulence
of melons and tomatoes, I
choose them all and place them
in my cart. A drift of herbs
floats by. I study orchestrated
labels then hurry past healthy
chunks of meat, flagrant sausages,
heaps of naked chicken thighs,
and glistening mounds of fish.
My cart full, I drive back home,
carry in packages shouting *Behold!*
I will make magic and transform
these groceries into a miracle for you.
A slab of Brie becomes the edge
of a receding glacier, eggs
extinguished stars, scallions
whips of comets; bottles
reflect dim ages of water,
carrots explode into flames,
radishes store memories,
tea bags store messages;
vanilla becomes a drop of sleep,
this box of salt an act of love.

Eve's Legacy

I pick the perfect one,
almost out of reach,
more tempting than the rest.
Then wedge my thumb
into the soft stem end,
twist and crack it in half,
its white skin umber at the core.

Stripped of other appetites,
I smell, nuzzle, tongue,
sink my teeth into the flesh,
rotating as I bite until
I reach the womb-shaped heart,
convinced that only a solid
piece of fruit understands
teeth that go on biting and
biting a whole lifetime.

It Is Enough

It is enough to lean against
the fabric of your flesh.
It is enough to lie
in the domestic morning.

It is enough to watch light
expand through windows
rising and falling
between our bodies on this bed,
this room, this continent.

We grow wise watching leaky faucets,
faded wallpaper, mismatched socks.
The coffee boiling on the stove
prepares us for the network news,
shopping malls, miracle cures,
and tomorrow always sitting on our bed.

But in this rush of years,
we have not lost the pure imagined past,
the here-it-is, the pitch, the pinnacle
of time shining from within a million
summers, or the music so intense it disappears.

We invent a lifetime out of small things,
free the air between our fingers,
diagram the stars, dream them into
daylight, and admit the future
which is here, always here
like a clock that runs forever.

Perspectives

under the breast of sky you move
in the wake of the lead car
on a low stretch of miles
through the country of your life

and watch the world happening
in a procession of car windows
and little hums of the heart

in summer's traffic
winds sift and blow the dust
and drift of years like dried leaves

visions of old loves
rise like steam from mist
the wheel holds its own

you drive along the highway
from one exit to the next
the sky repeats old sunsets

the moon declares
its size   its weight
its serious intentions

tires spin on hard ground
toward a straight horizon
light rests on your reflection

and all the faces facing you are yours

Detour

she pilots the car
up the cracked driveway
into the street

after the stop sign
she changes her face and
pulls into her other life

every street's a new language
with purple mouths of lilacs
trees crowding horizons
and mountains hanging in chains

with a hand delivered
from all heaviness she
steers the car while her
shadow on the windshield
waits like an older sister

the road snakes ahead
up the mountain
tires hissing like wings
steadily away from the earth

she's looking for a place
where she can hear
prologues of sun and rain
where the dark eye of night closes
where rivers have no permanent addresses

she's looking for her wild-weed children
all bark and twigs
chirping through summer
just about to become

she's looking for the point
where clock and compass meet
then she'll sit in antique darkness
drinking wine
staring at the Pacific
its waves drowning in salt and secrets

she knows distance and numbers
divide memory by half
and by the time she's old
there will be nothing left to remember
so she sits in silence
the seat beside her empty
and watches the sky unwind

Time Lag

The star I see,
the light my eyes reflect,
that crystal globe
extinguished long ago
is now a traveler in time
translating distances
between the star that was
and I who am.

But if I love you now,
you cannot possibly love me.
Whatever heat you contained
cooled in your long flight.
And what began that journey
has come and gone
long before I knew you.

But in love's sweet logic,
I stretch across
steep registers,
broad intervals of time,
unsung territories
until we reach and touch
defying all the laws.

Letting Go

he stalks them
clockwise
around the pond
an old hunter
happy in pursuit of

frogs
full of muscle and mucous
in thick sacks of skin
squatting on swampy ground
croaking gutturals

in their wet world
of fat summer air
tangled roots
and sun coating the pond's surface
with pools of liquid honey

he sneaks up
pounces
captures

carries his victim
in his mouth
halfway around

game ends
he spits it out
watches it leap
back
into the water

this old dog
follows the ritual
of catch-and-release
does what he knows
how to do

and we too
learn to gauge
the necessary distance
between loving
and letting go

The Fox

She patrols the shadows.
I separate sounds that enter
from sounds that leave.

Driven from the woods, she
moves in solitary circles
around the house
propelled by hunger.

As she devours apples,
I wipe froth from my mouth
and feel the pulse of wild things
in the night of the forest.

The smallest rasp of leaf on leaf
is signal enough to sense a victim,
to make the perfect strike
in a linkage of dreams.

When she trots off,
brush extended, she turns
for one last look at me.

From the door, half open,
I return that look,
staring the wilderness down.

Route 6

On Route 6, I hit a squirrel.
It danced like a windblown leaf
but the car behind left few choices:
a small broken shape
or the ditch.

The body trembled.
I stopped the car,
ran over to make certain.
It was dead.

Cleanup crews
do their job
and woods are overflowing
with fresh life
and wild

but I listen
for the sound of wheels
crunching

and the suddenness.

This Town

This town is small enough
to fill a single snapshot,
only a post office,
gas station, and two
liquor stores, both held up
last Thursday by men with

sawed-off double-barrel
shotguns. In the first,
they scooped up the take,
eighty dollars.
In the next, the clerk fired
his brand new gun.

This town is welded together
by silence. Here,
the government pheasants
surrender to the bullet,
the cattle to the milking machine,
and the open window
to the smell of manure.

Winter is a frosted lens
of sky where only eyes
are travelers, spring
the bronzed belly
of the first selectman
painting the same iron bridge
year after year.

Summer is a pond full of
catfish and larger fish
tasting of mud,
autumn a hunter aiming

a gun at what we've
never understood but
choose to love.

In this town, stone walls
bear witness against each other.

What Happens

Snow adds another layer
to the year, and silence
continues to arrive as
though we lived on the back
porch of time where the milk-
man forgets to collect
his bottles.

              But around
the corner of April,
spring rushes in, and
the everyday happens.
A door slams,
a glass shatters

              and from
an open window a radio
is breaking someone's
heart. We wake into
morning with

              the sun
smiling like a tour guide
willing to sell us
the rest of the trip.
We buy it,

wear our
morning face, walk out
into an absence of
fences and the sky
precisely blue.

At work
we sharpen pencils
to their vanishing points,
measure the chairness
of a chair, the tenacity
of rubber bands and
paper clips.

When day
whittles down, we come
back home to evening
meals, conversations
mixing metaphors with
onions, and as

light fades,
we sit breathless
waiting for the unknown
to be discovered.

Like an Ideal Tenant

Like an ideal tenant
the bullet fits precisely in the wound,
closer than a friend,
a relative, a lover.
Removing it, what can we
give the body in exchange
to accommodate it
half so well?

Always the unexpected caller,
it only sleeps with strangers,
never fails to find the perfect host,
and in turn becomes the perfect guest,
bringing no gift but itself,
demanding nothing.

Lying cradled in flesh,
never struggling to emerge,
cushioned in that hollow
as if it knew each curve,
it wraps itself in silence.

Suspended

In a corner catching pond shade,
there's a fraction of space
where dark beginnings are stored.

Something moves in an elegant line
like the passage of a star in slow
motion surging back to earlier, wilder

springs or far ahead to unknown
autumns. My temperature cools.
I'm still tethered to the planet

counting stars splintering the sky,
confirming that the universe won't
vanish nor will I reappear. Silence

stretches like a live wire over unexpected
lengths of time. Suspended in a life
I never enter or leave, I walk

with country feet through hours of easy
quiet. Something always happens. Dead
leaf and live seed drift down together.

Sky practices for winter. Water hums music
under air's loose skin. Hours slip off without
my knowing, and the world is twice as far away.

Safe Distance

Something lies half buried, waiting.
Silence has its holding place in cracks,
crevices, erosions. On overgrown corners,
thistles raise their spears, rocks their humps.
Weeds tighten roots in a stranglehold.
Vines twist through rotting lumber to crown
the house before the slow return, beyond lines
of shatter, back to a dream of animals again.

Hidden from the world in a couch of grass
and leaves, secure from storms that pass, I
depend on old migrations, a slow measuring
of ends, and where blindness leads, I follow.
Aboveground scrub grass bristles, and the scent
of danger's everywhere, but I know how safe
a safe distance under earth is and how far.

I'd Like to Color Myself Calm

I'd like to color myself calm
in a shade so subtle
it could not be seen
like hoarfrost outlining
limbs of birches
fog merging with winter weather
a shadow led by its own dark.

I'd like to color myself quiet
in tones rare and thin
like a seedling's feathered sprout
a filament of light threading
into the slender motions of sleep
shades of dark that women wear when they awake.

I'd like to color myself cool
on the white rim of night,
cup the day in my hands,
feel its glowing flame
fold back, burn out,
raise my shadow to its proper height.
Then, hidden in the foliage
of darkness, I'd become
everything I ever looked upon.

Writing Space

This house distilled from
time invites me in.
My dents are everywhere.
The chair I sit in,
the desk I work at
occupy the area
I once imagined.

Desk,
chair
slide into place,
the width, the breadth,
a perfect accommodation.

The room inside my private room
holds a wide slice
of tight-blue sky
and a sweet apple of light.

There,
I feel the peace
of pen and paper.

Writing letters
with indelible ink, I
trace an A for you,
S for sons,
H for home

smear them with my fingertips
taste their salty sweetness
feel their scratch and stroke.

I watch words vanish
off the page making room
for more and hear the silence
between sentences.

Framed by narrow margins
they know their limit,
and I, within the
boundaries of this room
and these four walls,
know mine.

Messages

scrubbed autumn days
afternoons smelling of smoke
a few leaves clinging to branches
curl like fortune cookies
hiding the same messages
year after year

the sun defines
a knee print in the grass
an elbow of earth
an armful of shade

we smell the dust
the weeds   the weather
as pebbles in our palms
sift back to sand

the current drags the day
from one shore to another
tonight it will snow
tomorrow it will melt

we follow the direction
of our feet   the inclination
of our heads as stars
obey their own astronomies

Quiet As Sand

I rub my hand across your chest
so gently neither of us
feels it   we breath
in and out of focus   limbs
whisper against sheets

the moon spreads
its chalky glow   we hear
wind scouring trees
leaves rubbing
smooth skinned
against each other

after small silences
we breathe
each other in
and see the dark
unravel

everything exactly
where it is
the house   the fence

the spine of earth
we're somewhere we've
always been before

all night the unknown
waits to be discovered
when dawn drifts in
quiet as sand
I say good-bye
to all my ghosts
throw open windows

sunlight melts
on my hands and wild geese
ladder the sky   I hear
the stroke of grass on grass
as morning makes an entrance
with fanfares of light
on the rim of the world

Fuel

Fragments of the old world
twist loose like ash from fire
taking us back to wood-
stoves and logs piled high
at the kitchen door.

We walk the woods and mark
the trees for fuel.
Axes biting into timber
recall my father hacking
away at ninety years

always against the grain
fighting the vacancy
in which his time was measured.
He'd heft the logs to weigh

the warmth each offered
in that bare time
when nothing grew and
weather was everywhere.

After the sawing, splitting, stacking
just the way he taught us,
we kneel, count the rings,
the slow inscription of years

to fuel such a life as his
measured, muscular,
different from all others.

Inventions

I'd reinvent that house on Burrows
a block from the police station,
the wooden streetcar, and the north wind
slicing into us at Portage Avenue and Main.

I'd reinvent long Sunday afternoons,
frost sharpening its claws on telephone wires,
snow lying wet and heavy, my breath making
perfect circles on the icy windowpane.

I'd reinvent steamy summer days
when the wax fruit lost its shape;
we'd lie in the long grass of August,
sweat covering us like a second skin.

Older now, I'm free of all inventions
but on early morning walks something moves
beside me whispering my other name,
reminding me of trees glittering with
hoarfrost, northern lights, an electric
moon, and the sparkling tundra of the past.

Things

have their own lives here.
The radio spins
to its favorite program;
the staircase slows down
to one half-step at a time.

A grey glaze coats the house
and in the wild anarchy of kitchens
windows ration light
clocks stop long enough to chime
graters peel skin from vegetable lives.

As sound percolates the stillness
I pour soft scrubbings
through my hands
and listen to the blood-rush
the same old circuitry.

Then in the brute
blaze of noon, I'll
eat my baked potato
in my buttered world.

Basic

In the distance, a tractor driven
by a brushstroke of a man
weaves across the fields
finely balanced on the sill
of the world. At dusk
barns and fences grow invisible.
Crickets count the seconds.

He knows it all:
spring, operatic and sudden
summer's sweaty embrace
autumn's clutter of leaves
winter, holding hard and white.

Then, with a shrug
as natural as apples lying
hearts up on the ground,
he accepts the long dying
and the sudden one.

Driftwood Days

A shaft of light slips
through a patch of
sky worn thin with winter.

Air thick with cold, winds
press hard against the house
in days of driftwood courage.

Silence stretches over
trees deepening to charcoal,
fence posts iced by frost,
barns sere and weather scorched.

Memories layer the air,
a dream of summer afternoons
when the sun honeyed
the earth and things came

softly to order. Now, with no
time left, the landscape pares
down to a bird sitting on a limb,
silent as bark, almost invisible.

She

rummages through the alphabet
for friends
names of her brothers
the sound of her own voice
fragile with distance

files away the past
alphabetically
checks the stove
turns off the lights
and comes late to her mother's funeral

talks to death
like a next-door neighbor
listens to the hours grinding their gears
and counts days
detaching themselves like loose buttons

barricades the door
watches for trees exploding
waters rising
assassins cruising the streets
and night hovering dangerous and close

Her Silence

Swollen with shapes
and sounds of all
her children, how
did she shrink so quickly?

What happened to her hair
that she must keep it
hidden underneath
a kerchief or a wig?

Did she lose it
from a childhood illness
or tear it by the roots
when her oldest drowned?

No one listened
to her stories, just
a few old ladies who
had heard them all

before and wouldn't listen
anyway, they had their
own stories waiting.
One by one, the old

shapes grew dim and
disappeared. She could no
longer thread her needle
or hear the front door slam.

I move across the continent
back to heavy snows and
the warm kitchen where her sighs
fall from every crack

in the plaster, covering me
with thin layers of sound
until I become her shadow.
Following her to places

in a time before my time,
I have just begun
to understand the language
of her silence.

Night Song

After slashing through our jungle
full of savage summer
where animals lie sick
with heat (even the hunters
too overcome to drag
trophies home), we'll dream
through scorched nights
of cool vegetable mornings,
corn springing from
the navel of Osiris,
the Nile emptying drop by
drop into a glass of milk.

Inheritance

You laughed when I demanded souvenirs,
the antimacassars greasy with hair oil,
a crystal shot glass my father used on Fridays
filled with whiskey beneficial for his heart.

I wanted stories half heard, half remembered,
the names of relatives long dead,
the curses you showered on us
when we were late for school,
and the barley soup still growing in my plate.

You hugged me like the summer holidays.
You never warned me there might come a time.
You only told me death was not my business
and departure meant return was certain.

Ma, you lied.

The Outer Edge

The blind
whisper to each other
in rinsed voices.

They ask me to describe
darkness. I begin
with the charred edge

of the sea, winds trapped
in caves, a wheel turning
away from itself.

I have gone
into the hollow place
behind my eyes,

to the outer edge
of sight moving
on white lizard feet.

No longer blinded
by the visible, the world
is nearer in the dark.

Light sinks
inward to its core
and the wind

on its ghost crutch
brushes the limits of a star.

Back

Back
reversing the flow
back through the looking glass
up from the rabbit hole
in from out there.

Back
into the stunned silence
of snow, a grey quiet,
a stripping clean to the roots
and our breath making perfect circles.

Back
to Main Street
with summer twilight
spreading like fire in dry grass,
the soft susurrus of a slow leak in the day.

My hands
stretching like antennae,
now in this street
now in that.

Back
to wrap that child's universe
around me once again
and warm this woman's frame.

Still Here

Our faces all sky
and air. Breeze
resting on bare shoulders,
the family's side by
side in a photograph
slightly out of focus.

I spent my whole life
fitting into those pictures,
cramped a little but
all parts reconciled
without an arm cut off
or my body ending at the knee.

Now, I'm taking snapshots
framed with my own designs.
In this new setting,
light crayons the window,

the sky's a rich blue glaze,
California's sprawling
in the sun, and I'm intact—
no amputations—

staring at that face
in the mirror, whispering,
You're still here,
and smiling
as if I'd won a prize.

Holding Time in Check

I wipe the table clean
prop a paperback on the sugar bowl
and dream of Sunday afternoons
with the *New York Times* and
everyone hiking the Nipmuk Trail
or listening to Bach.

Leaving home, road open
all the way to the sky,
the distance never changed from where
I'd been to where I was.

I've left behind old houses filled with dust
the dull electric burn of chicken coops
children playing ghost in folds of snow
and days gone grey with calm.
Years vanish into mirrors
holding time in check.

In Safeway aisles we say *nice day*
as neon grins blink off and on.
The air is sweet and soft
in afternoons on long walks
through arabesques of flowers.
On Saturdays the phone's blue ring is
a bird note of *hello*.

Everyone's accounted for
and no one died today.

Penicillin

If the bread box gives off memories
of that laboratory on Spadina Avenue
and the bread becomes a special shade of green,
don't throw it out. In honor of

Sir Alexander Fleming, let it be.
That mold's a miracle, and if it
smells, so much the better. Strong
cures give off strong smells.

In my singing season when I passed
that building twice a day, I was
safe inside a charmed circle
still protecting me.

Although I carry deep inside
a medley of strong fumes—
garlic to ward off polio,
mustard plasters for pneumonia,
fish oil to make me live a hundred years—
none have the magic properties
of Alexander Fleming's mold.

It holds the flavor of conservatory
corridors, floodlights, applause,
my own special mailbox.
And lately, it reminds me
of quick springs, slow autumns,
my mouth singing in the winter.

Reminders

rusty sky stretched
tight as barbed wire
snow combing itself
against the house
wind tossing a lost sneaker
nudging a memory of children

in furrows of snow
traps of spring are set
silt and grit of moments
moving thickly through
the oven of summer
robins shuttling from tree to tree
dandelions spewing white heads
children walking backward
with sun-painted hands

their absence now
like a gouge in the snow
as drifts expose
reminders
earth-stained
weatherworn
their discards
our inheritance

Each Night

I revolve past your sleep
and see your darker outlines
against the window,
a mountain of quilt,
a trail outlining the long foothills.
The heart pounds at this altitude.
I take short, quick breaths matching yours.
Safe in this high country,
I lie here in layered white,
folding into you beside me
in the hairspring intervals
between dark and light.

Meltdown

I was perfectly
suspended in winter's isolation,
wrapped in my body's warmth,
secure in my own keeping,
and you,
perfect in your condition;
both of us poised
toward each other,
frozen in our certainty
and having known
exactly what it was to be
cold and separate and sure,
we chose to melt.

Discovery

Following the icy spine
of winter into the woods, I'm
deep in the silence of animals
and the lifeless breathing of snow.

In summer when air flows like saffron,
I follow a whisper in the tall grass,
a signal flashing from the hedge,
a shadow pulsing in the pond.

At night, I follow the tracks
you plow in the sheets
where your body preserves
the light of leaves long-buried.

But your dark animal
in its protective coat of sleep
prowls away to places
I cannot follow.

Ordinary Things

People we do not know
move all around us.
When they leave
there is no one.

We live as quiet as a photograph
self-contained
mindful of our limits.

Here is the door.
Here the window.
Here the air between them.

We stir the soup
heat the house
rake leaves   shovel snow.

And it is always morning.
And it is always evening.
And it is always now.

Ancient Rounds

I wake early, climb
the oak's thick trunk
up to its sweet armpits.

The long night fades
like an image
on an ancient wall.

No one looks for me
under canopies of light
or rituals of rain.

The year makes perfect circles,
snow scented, leaf smoked,
a blending of decays

that spin me back.
Again I'm short-sleeved in
October, snowbound in December.

Again I'm seventeen and old
and wise as all of womankind.

A Temporary Visitor

My hand is shaped exactly like my hand.
My fingers move like fingers
not like a white spider
or hermit crab.

My voice is exactly like my voice
not a musical invention
or sound wrapped in silence.

My body is only my body
not a receptacle for light
or a shade invading the dark.

I am not an hourglass
with sand trickling through.
I am only a padded skeleton,
a temporary visitor.

Unfinished Business

The unfinished business between us
postponed, now content to lie against
each other in perfect isolation,
a pair of ordinary bodies
with nothing sudden here,
and when the strong pulse
of morning beats against us,
the strange grows familiar again.

In rituals from other lives, we
grope our way downstairs
as though that walk would
cut our feet on toys abandoned
long ago and once again
ease into chairs, lean
on the table heavy with the weight
of earlier breakfasts.

The surface cleared,
the house swept clean
and empty of our sons,
in the near-perfect silence
of winter speech, we
shrug into our sweatered lives,
wrap them loose around us
and wear our passion lightly.

Search

I walk in—no one knows I'm there—
close the torn screen door, move
through the kitchen where something's
always bubbling on the stove, and find them
in the dining room, reading, playing cards,
pasting pictures of old movie stars on
unpainted walls. A dead man sings
"Pagliacci" on the windup gramophone.

Mother's out in back hanging up the wash
because it's always Monday, Father's
in his bathing suit lugging pails of water
from the pump, Brother's in the outhouse
reading last week's funnies, and the next-
door boy bangs nails in our roof. But I'm
looking for that nine-year-old building sand
castles in a made-up country at the beach.

She's the one I've come for. Her days
run together in one sunstruck afternoon.
I'm here to borrow it, to soak in the heat,
swim out to the pier, skip stones over
water, or lie loose and easy wasting
time. For this, I would give up
all my other lives.

Promise

I say *Yes* to the peeling away of winter,
to rain's slanted messages,
and the language of warm winds.

Yes to yeasty roots burrowing in earth,
to skeletal trees putting on flesh,
to ground smearing itself with lime-yellow pigment.

Yes to light quickening its pulse
and the sun blooming in our bodies
with a promise more permanent than love.

Yes to the unborn waiting to be born,
to the sky stretching naked overhead,
and the days so compact and clear,
I could carry them in my arms.

Threshold

I hold the oldest word I know
cupped in my hand
smooth as stone
warmed by the sun.
I rub it gently, but it
won't release its secret.

Last night it kissed me
on the lips, kept me
company a while
as I fed it, held it
up to the light
before letting go.

Today I move
from room to room
going nowhere.

Fragment by fragment
I gather thin
membranes of sound
and whatever knocks
I say

Come in.

About the Author

Ruth Daigon spent most of her life in the extreme climates of Winnipeg, Toronto, New York, and Connecticut where her primary activity was singing as a Columbia Recording Artist, a guest artist on CBS's *Camera Three,* a soloist with the New York Pro Musica, and in concert and recital appearances. When she sang at Dylan Thomas's funeral, she never dreamed that poetry would take over her life. Her collaboration with W.H. Auden to record Renaissance poetry and music for Columbia Records also gave no hint of what was to come—editing *Poets On:,* now in its twentieth year, contributing to major poetry journals, and winning national awards. It was on the East Coast where she made the transition from concert soprano to full-time poet/editor. She has since published three poetry collections: *Learning Not to Kill You* (Selkirk Press, 1975), *On My Side of the Bed* (Omnation Press, 1982), and *A Portable Past* (Realities Library Contemporary Poets Series, 1986). She now lives in the warmth of California's Bay Area where she continues to write, edit, and wait for the next future to arrive.

Papier-Mache Press

At Papier-Mache Press, it is our goal to identify and success-fully present important social issues through enduring works of beauty, grace, and strength. Through our work we hope to encourage empathy and respect among diverse communities, creating a bridge of understanding between the mainstream audience and those who might not otherwise be heard. We appreciate you, our customer, and strive to earn your contin-ued support. We also value the role of the bookseller in achieving our goals. We are especially grateful to the many independent booksellers whose presence ensures a continuing diversity of opinion, information, and literature in our com-munities. We encourage you to support these bookstores with your patronage.

We publish many fine books about women's experiences. We also produce lovely posters and T-shirts that complement our anthologies. Please ask your local bookstore which Papier-Mache items they carry. To receive our complete catalog, send a self-addressed stamped envelope to Papier-Mache Press, 135 Aviation Way, #14, Watsonville, CA 95076, or call our toll-free number, 800-927-5913.